THE POWER OF 5AM

How Waking Up Early Can Transform Your Life and Boost Your Success

ERIC A. KATZ

THE POWER OF 5AM

*How Waking Up Early Can Transform Your Life
and Boost Your Success*

ERIC A. KATZ

Copyright © 2024 by ERIC A. KATZ All rights reserved.

No part of this publication may be reproduced, distributed, or transmitted in any form or by any means, including photocopying, recording, or other electronic or mechanical methods, without the prior written permission of the publisher, except in the case of brief quotations embodied in critical reviews and certain other non-commercial uses permitted by copyright law. This book is intended for personal use and educational purposes only. It is not permitted for resale or commercial distribution without the express permission of the copyright holder. For permission requests or inquiries, please contact the author at adepel80@gmail.com

Cover design in USA

Printed in USA

TABLE OF CONTENTS

Introduction

- The Power of Early Rising
- Why 5AM?
- How This Book Will Help You

Chapter 1: The Science Behind Waking Up Early

- The Biology of Early Mornings
- How Waking Up at 5AM Affects Your Brain and Productivity
- The Connection Between Sleep and Success

Chapter 2: Benefits of Waking Up at 5AM

- Improved Mental Clarity and Focus
- Enhanced Creativity and Problem-Solving
- Increased Productivity and Time Management
- Better Physical and Mental Health

Chapter 3: How to Make Waking Up at 5AM a Habit

- Setting Your Intention and Commitment
- Gradual Adjustments to Your Sleep Schedule
- Overcoming the Initial Struggles of Waking Up Early

Chapter 4: Designing Your Morning Routine

- The Power of Rituals and Routines
- Crafting a Morning Routine That Works for You
- Examples of Successful 5AM Routines

Chapter 5: How 5AM Can Impact Your Personal and Professional Life

- Using the Morning Hours to Focus on Personal Growth
- Building a Stronger Career and Achieving Goals
- The Power of Quiet Time for Deep Work

Chapter 6: Overcoming Common Challenges

- Combatting Morning Fatigue and Lack of Motivation
- How to Stay Consistent and Avoid Burnout
- Adjusting Your Routine During Life's Unexpected Events

Chapter 7: Transforming Your Life Through Consistency

- Tracking Progress and Celebrating Small Wins
- The Compound Effect of Early Rising Over Time
- Stories of Individuals Who Transformed Their Lives by Embracing 5AM

Conclusion

- The Long-Term Benefits of Waking Up Early
- Your Next Steps to Becoming a Morning Master
- Final Words of Encouragement

DISCLAIMER

The information provided in this eBook, *"The Power of 5AM: How Waking Up Early Can Transform Your Life and Boost Your Success:"* is intended for general guidance and informational purposes only. While every effort has been made to ensure accuracy, travel conditions, prices, and regulations may change over time, and the author does not guarantee the completeness or current validity of the information contained herein. Readers are advised to conduct their own research or consult relevant local authorities or travel services before making any travel decisions. The author and publisher assume no liability for any loss, injury, or inconvenience experienced as a result of information presented in this guide. All travel decisions are made at the reader's discretion and risk.

INTRODUCTION

There's something magical about the early hours of the day. There is a particular silence that feels sacrosanct and unspoiled before the world awakens. Many of the most successful people in the world have found their best productivity, creativity, and clarity at this time. They've uncovered a secret—an unexplored reservoir of potential that is located just past sunrise. It's the power of rising early and a habit that may change your life in ways you never would have thought possible.

People have been praising the benefits of rising early for millennia. Although it is frequently used as a straightforward axiom, the saying "the early bird catches the worm" has a deeper meaning. This advice has persisted throughout history for a reason: getting up early gives you a distinct advantage over other people. It's not only about being productive, though; it's also about using those peaceful morning hours to establish the tone for the remainder of the day and, eventually, your life. This is where 5 AM's strength resides.

The Power of Early Rising
You are given something valuable in the quiet of the early morning: time. Distraction-free time. Time before your surroundings get chaotic, before your phone is inundated with notifications, before the incessant din of work, social commitments, and daily life starts to take over. Your mind is free and clear in these early hours. Your attention is not being demanded, rushed, or under pressure. You can give yourself, your objectives, and your personal development your whole attention at this point.

Having more time in your day is not the only benefit of rising early. Quality is more important than quantity. One of the most productive times of the day is in the morning. You're not just starting a new day when you get up early; you're also laying the groundwork for everything that comes after. Your mind is clear, your energy is renewed, and you can focus on the things that really count. This is your time to mold, and if you utilize it wisely, it can cause significant changes in your life.

Our brains function best in the early hours of the morning, according to studies. The stress hormone cortisol is stronger in the morning, which aids with concentration and alertness. We are better able to make decisions, have more creative freedom, and are more inclined to take on difficult jobs head-on. Additionally, early risers have more regular habits, and consistency produces long-lasting effects. The advantages of rising early extend beyond a busy morning; they lay the groundwork for achievement, development, and overall wellbeing in all facets of life.

The reality is that not everyone finds it easy to get up early. It calls for a change of perspective and a dedication to putting your future and well-being first. Making the most of those early hours and utilizing them to further your objectives is more important than simply rising early. Here's where the magic takes place.

Why 5 AM?
Why, then, at 5 AM? Why not simply get up a little later or an hour earlier? What's so great about this hour in particular? In actuality, there are a number of reasons why 5 AM is the ideal time to wake up.

First of all, it's early enough that you can enjoy the morning's peace and quiet without feeling hurried. You won't have to contend with the bustle of the outside world if you get up at five in the morning. You have a good chunk of time to yourself, and the distractions haven't yet appeared. You can start your day slowly at 5 AM without feeling rushed to get started. It's a time to take care of oneself, whether that means exercising, meditating, or just spending a few minutes making plans for the day.

Second, you have enough time to complete important activities before the outside world starts clamoring for your attention if you get up at five in the morning. The rest of the world is starting to awaken by 7 or 8 AM, and your day is beginning to fill up with obligations, meetings, phone calls, and emails. However, you've already had two hours of uninterrupted, concentrated time to accomplish tasks if you get up at five in the morning. That's two more hours to work on your health, creative endeavors, personal objectives, or anything else that matters to you. You can work deeply and meaningfully during this period without being distracted.

The fact that 5 AM gets you a head start on the remainder of the day is another factor contributing to its potency. You're giving yourself a competitive advantage by rising at five in the morning. You're setting the tone for the remainder of the day by beginning it with focus and purpose. You've already achieved something important while others are still asleep or just beginning to wake up. You may feel more confident and fulfilled throughout the day as a result of this sense of success, which can also generate good momentum.

Finally, 5 AM is the ideal time to establish a productive morning routine. It's crucial in the first hour after waking up. Your body and mind are most open to forming new habits at this time. Making deliberate use of this time can help you develop successful and healthy habits that last a lifetime. 5 AM is the best time to lay the groundwork for a successful and satisfying day, whether it be through journaling, exercise, meditation, or day planning.

How This Book Will Help You
You might be asking how you can truly make this change in your life now that you know the benefits of rising early and why 5 AM

is such a transformational time. This book fills that need. In order to help you make the most of the early morning hours and use them to build the life you've always desired, The Power of 5AM: How Waking Up Early Can Transform Your Life and Boost Your Success was written.

This book will teach you how to wake up at five in the morning and how to develop a routine that works for you. I'll walk you through the science of early mornings and how they impact your body, mind, and productivity. We'll discuss the advantages of rising early, such as improved health and creativity, and I'll demonstrate how to create a daily routine that will help you succeed.

Additionally, this book will assist you in overcoming the typical obstacles that many individuals have when attempting to become an early riser. I'll offer helpful advice and techniques to assist you make the shift easily and effectively, whether you're struggling with procrastination, morning weariness, or a new sleep routine. In order to increase productivity and accomplish your goals, both personal and professional, you will also learn how to maintain consistency, monitor your progress, and make the most of your early mornings.

This work is ultimately about change. It's about taking back your mornings and making the most of them to reach your greatest potential. You're taking charge of your life by rising early and deliberately planning your mornings. You're prioritizing yourself, positioning yourself for achievement, and building the momentum required to realize your goals. You can harness the power of 5 AM, and this book will show you just how to do it.

Getting up at five in the morning can have a significant impact on your life, whether your goal is to increase your creativity, productivity, or health, or just to live a more balanced and satisfying existence. Together, let's go on this adventure and change your mornings and your life, one day at a time.

The foundation for a path of transformation is laid forth in this introduction. I'm hoping it aligns with the goal you have for your book. Tell me if there is anything you would like changed!

CHAPTER ONE

THE SCIENCE BEHIND WAKING UP EARLY

Early mornings have traditionally been linked to success, productivity, and personal development. However, there is a strong scientific basis that explains why rising early can have such a significant impact on our lives, going beyond anecdotal evidence and conventional wisdom. The intricate cycles of our bodies, biology, and brain are the foundations of the research underlying early wakefulness. Knowing this information will inspire you to make 5 AM a non-negotiable part of your routine and help you recognize the power of the early hours. Let's examine how our biology cooperates to make rising early an essential success strategy.

The Biology of Early Mornings
The circadian rhythm is a natural internal clock that controls our bodies. This roughly 24-hour cycle controls a number of our physiological functions, such as hormone synthesis, body temperature, and the sleep-wake cycle. A major component in determining when we feel most awake and when we feel most fatigued is the circadian rhythm, which is controlled by external variables, namely light and darkness.

The circadian rhythm, sometimes known as our body's "biological clock," is intricately linked to the day-night cycles of the planet. Our predecessors' sleep schedules in prehistoric times were mostly controlled by the sun's rise and set. The human brain began to become attentive as the sun rose, and the body's natural mechanisms took over. On the other hand, the body started getting ready for sleep when the sun went down.

Our circadian rhythms can be distorted by the artificial lights and displays that surround us in modern times, making it more difficult to maintain the natural cycles of sleep and wakefulness. Fatigue, trouble sleeping, and other health concerns might result from this disturbance. But the research is clear: we may access a deeper, more productive energy if we can synchronize our waking hours with the earth's natural rhythms.

Our bodies are frequently primed for alertness and focus when we get up early, especially around five in the morning. The first few hours after waking up are among the most concentrated and productive times of the day, according to research. We get an energy boost in the morning because the body naturally raises cortisol levels, which are linked to stress but also attentiveness. We approach jobs with clarity thanks to this natural energy boost, and we are more focused than we are later in the day when distractions and mental exhaustion begin to accumulate.

How Waking Up at 5 AM Affects Your Brain and Productivity
Having additional hours in the day is not the only benefit of rising at five in the morning. Your brain is operating at its best when you get up early. The brain is less crowded and yet fresh in the early hours of the day. Our brains are most capable of focusing, being creative, and solving problems in the early hours of the morning. The calm of the morning somehow makes it easier for our thoughts to reach higher cognitive capacities.

According to neuroscience research, the brain can focus and concentrate more better in the morning than it can at any other time of day. This is because the information overload that tends to build up throughout the day is still mostly absent from our minds. The brain is constantly processing sensory information, making judgments, and balancing tasks throughout the day. Mental tiredness brought on by this continuous mental activity makes it more difficult to focus or do in-depth work.

However, there are fewer distractions in the early morning. The needs of the day have not yet materialized, and the world remains silent. Because of this, the early hours of the morning are perfect for intense, concentrated work. You're allowing your brain to do this deep work when you wake up at five in the morning, whether it's introspection, solving a challenging problem, or working on a creative endeavor. The ability of the brain to maintain a state of flow, which results in increased focus and productivity, is improved.

The control of neurotransmitters in the brain is one of the main elements that leads to this enhanced productivity. Neurotransmitters that affect motivation, mood, and focus include dopamine, serotonin, and norepinephrine. Early in the morning, these molecules are automatically regulated, providing us with the mental energy to begin tasks requiring focus. These hormones combine to increase our drive and decrease the chance of procrastination when we rise early.

The impact of early waking on decision-making is another significant element. The prefrontal cortex, which is in charge of planning and decision-making, is more active and our brains are clearer when we wake up at five in the morning. We are better able to establish priorities, make critical decisions, and intentionally plan our days as a result. Making decisions gets harder as the day wears on and mental exhaustion sets in. We can prevent this weariness and make the best choices when it counts most by getting up early.

The Connection Between Success and Sleep
Although getting up early is a great strategy for success, it's crucial to understand that it functions best when combined with restful sleep. There is no denying the link between achievement and sleep.

The basis of our mental and physical health is sleep. The body and brain undergo vital processes of renewal and repair while we sleep. But not all sleep is made equal, and how well you sleep has a significant influence on how successful and productive you are during the day.

For optimal health, mood control, and cognitive performance, a restful night's sleep is essential. The brain processes emotions, organizes memories, and eliminates pollutants as you sleep deeply. Our brains are maintained during this time, so when we wake up, we are alert, focused, and prepared to face the day. We suffer from slower reaction times, diminished memory retention, and cognitive impairments when we don't get enough good sleep. Chronic sleep deprivation over time can result in major health problems like depression, obesity, and heart disease.

However, what role does sleep play in the early-morning equation? Balance is crucial. Making sleep a priority and making sure you're getting enough sleep are crucial if you want to be able to wake up at five in the morning every day. Most individuals should aim for seven to nine hours of sleep every night. You will need to go to bed earlier in order to get enough sleep if you wake up at five in the morning.

One advantage of rising early is that it makes you reassess your sleeping patterns. It takes discipline to get up at five in the morning, and you'll also need to modify your nightly routine to make the early rise efficient. This could entail reducing screen time, developing a more calming nighttime routine, and preparing your body for sleep. Setting an early wake-up time will inevitably result in better sleep, which will enhance your productivity, mental clarity, and cognitive performance.

Additionally, people who rise early are typically more aware of their sleep schedules. They are aware that getting up at five in the morning is ineffective unless they deliberately establish a sleep schedule that facilitates it. In this sense, getting up early can result in improved sleep hygiene, which further impacts achievement.

In conclusion
There is much scientific support for getting up early. Aligning your body with its natural rhythms, making the most of the early hours when your brain is most focused, and utilizing that time to be productive, creative, and intentional are more important than simply having more hours in the day. When you get up early and give your body the rest it needs, you unlock a level of potential that lays the groundwork for long-term success. This makes the link between sleep, the circadian rhythm, and productivity evident. Early waking is a statistically supported strategy that can help you accomplish more in less time with more clarity and purpose, but it is not a panacea.

As you start the habit of rising at five in the morning, keep in mind that it's not just about the time on the clock; it's also about the psychological, emotional, and physical advantages of adjusting your schedule to your body's natural cycles. Consistently adopting the powerful habit of rising early can improve your general well-being, productivity, and success.

CHAPTER TWO

BENEFITS OF WAKING UP AT 5AM

Many people associate the thought of rising at five in the morning with tiresome alarm clocks and the confusing fog of the early hours of the day. However, many who adopt this pattern find that their lives undergo a significant change that goes far beyond just having more hours in the day. There are several advantages to arising at five in the morning, including a complete change in our perspective on productivity, mental clarity, creativity, and health in addition to giving us a head start on the day. This chapter examines how getting up early—especially at five in the morning—can significantly impact your success and quality of life.

Improved Mental Clarity and Focus
The increase in attention and mental clarity is among the most obvious advantages of rising around five in the morning. There is an unmatched chance for your mind to function without the interruptions that usually overtake our thoughts during the day in the stillness of the early morning while everyone else is still asleep. Because the brain is still recovering from a restful night's sleep, early risers frequently say that the first few hours after awakening are the most concentrated and cognitively clear. The body's circadian cycle, which encourages alertness and focus in the morning, is responsible for this clarity.

Your mind hasn't yet been overloaded with emails, phone calls, social media, and other distractions that vie for your attention throughout the day when you wake up at five in the morning. Your brain becomes more focused and productive when it is not burdened by outside distractions. You can use this time to work deeply, putting your best effort and precision into your most difficult activities. The early hours offer a degree of focus that is hard to duplicate once the daily grind takes over, whether you're writing, brainstorming, or solving a challenging problem.

The mind is also less prone to tiredness during these early hours. As we work, make decisions, and engage with others throughout the day, mental exhaustion starts to build up. Most people find it more difficult to remain motivated or concentrated by 5 PM. However, you can make the most of the period when your mind is at its most alert by rising early. Because your brain is still in a state of clarity, you may do more at this time of increased focus than you might in a few hours later in the day.

Enhanced Creativity and Problem-Solving
Beyond improving focus and mental clarity, getting up early has a major positive impact on creativity and problem-solving skills. Without the typical stresses and diversions of everyday life, the peace and quiet of the early morning allows your mind to roam, think freely, and explore new ideas. This quiet setting frequently fosters creativity since it allows you to use your imagination and see challenges from a different angle.

Your mind is free to make connections between concepts that you might not have thought of during the day in the morning. Moments of stillness, which the early morning provides, are often the sites of creative breakthroughs. You give yourself time to blog, meditate, or just reflect on your objectives, aspirations, and tasks when you wake up at five in the morning. This kind of introspective thinking is a crucial component of your creative process because it might generate fresh concepts and answers.

Early morning clarity and stillness are also beneficial for problem-solving. When confronted with a difficult problem, the tendency is to jump right in and attempt to find a quick solution. However, this haste might impair judgment and make it more difficult to make wise decisions. You offer yourself the chance to face issues with composure by rising at five in the morning, which enables you to carefully consider your options and come up with creative solutions. This kind of thinking, which is based on originality and clarity, is what propels advancement on both a personal and professional level.

Increased Productivity and Time Management
Getting up at five in the morning has a significant effect on time management and productivity. You have an advantage over others who sleep in and start their day hurriedly because you have the entire day ahead of you. How you organize your early hours will determine how productive you are. Setting the tone for the rest of the day by rising early gives you the opportunity to concentrate on critical activities before work, family, and other commitments start to take over.

You can use the early morning hours, which are frequently unbroken, to finish work requiring in-depth concentration, preparation, or introspection. The time you spend in the morning lays the groundwork for a more effective and productive day, whether you're working on a project at work, planning your day, or advancing toward personal objectives. Because they are functioning at their best during those early hours, early risers frequently discover that they achieve more in the first few hours of the day than they would throughout the afternoon.

Getting up early also significantly improves time management. Getting up at five in the morning gives you the chance to organize your day, prioritizing chores and establishing objectives for your desired outcome. To stay on course and make sure you're working toward your most essential goals, you need to have a clear sense of purpose and direction. The responsibilities of the day might easily overwhelm you if you don't have a clear strategy, but getting up early enables you to be proactive rather than reactive.

Early risers also have a tendency to become more consistent and disciplined. Getting up at the same time each day creates a solid pattern that gives you more control over your schedule. When you establish a routine, you improve your ability to manage your workload, strike a balance between work and personal obligations, and make time for rest and self-care. Developing this time management skill through the practice of rising early makes it simpler to continue being productive without being overly exhausted or burned out.

Better Physical and Mental Health
Its beneficial effects on mental and physical health are arguably among the most significant advantages of rising at five in the morning. Getting up early allows you the time and space you need to take care of yourself, which is crucial for leading a balanced and healthy lifestyle. Getting up at five in the morning fosters behaviors like exercising, eating a good diet, and practicing mindfulness that improve physical health.

One of the most popular routines among early risers is working out first thing in the morning. Morning workouts, whether they involve jogging, yoga, or going to the gym, have been demonstrated to offer a host of health advantages. Exercise releases endorphins, the body's natural mood boosters, increases vitality, and strengthens the heart. You may enhance your attitude and motivation for the remainder of the day in addition to improving your health by include physical activity in your morning routine.

Getting up early also promotes mental health. Introspection, mindfulness, and meditation—activities that aid in lowering tension and anxiety—are made possible by the early silence. Getting up early gives you the opportunity to think, process, and express gratitude—all of which have been shown to improve mental health. According to studies, mindfulness exercises like meditation and deep breathing can enhance focus, reduce cortisol levels, and boost emotions of contentment.

Aside from these advantages, getting up early allows you to create a consistent sleep schedule. The discipline of rising early naturally results in earlier bedtimes, which guarantees that you obtain the recommended seven to nine hours of sleep per night. Sleep is essential for physical wellness. Immune system performance, cognitive function, and emotional fortitude are all significantly impacted by regular, restful sleep. You establish a balanced lifestyle that promotes long-term health and vigor by rising at five in the morning.

In conclusion
The advantages of rising at five in the morning are profound and impact many facets of your life, including your productivity, well-being, health, and mental clarity and creativity. A unique blend of opportunity, concentration, and tranquility that is hard to come by later in the day is provided by rising early. You offer yourself the gift of time when you get up early: time to think, plan, work out, and focus on the things that really important. You can accomplish your personal and professional goals more quickly, effectively, and effectively with the clarity, creativity, and productivity that come with rising at five in the morning. You may take charge of your life and put yourself on a path of development and success by adopting this habit, which will open up a new level of success and wellbeing.

CHAPTER THREE

HOW TO MAKE WAKING UP AT 5AM A HABIT

Getting up at five in the morning seems like a far-off fantasy to many people, something that only a handful with exceptional self-control and time management skills can accomplish. However, regardless of one's starting point, anyone can develop the practice of rising early. The purpose of the approach is to make a long-lasting lifestyle change that supports your individual objectives, not to impose yourself into a strict regimen. This chapter will discuss how to develop the habit of waking up at 5 AM, beginning with establishing your objective, gradually modifying your sleep routine, and overcoming the initial challenges that invariably arise with establishing a new habit.

Your commitment to waking up early needs to be unwavering. Setting a clear aim is the first step in developing the habit of waking up at five in the morning. Knowing why you want to get up early in the first place is crucial. When difficulties emerge or you are tempted to return to the comfort of your warm bed after a few days of rising early, it might be simple to give up without a compelling and obvious cause. Establishing your intention entails realizing that this new habit is a commitment to yourself and your objectives rather than merely a modification of your regular schedule.

Your goal ought to be strong and intimate. What do you want to achieve by rising early in the morning? Is it to have more time for personal development, exercise, or self-care? Do you wish to increase your output and accomplish your career objectives more quickly? Or would you want to have time for introspection, meditation, or a passion project that is frequently neglected throughout the day? Whatever your motivations, put them in writing and remember them the next time you want to press the snooze button.

You must be steadfast in your resolve to rise early. Recognize that developing this habit will take time and that it might not always be easy. You can overcome periods of uncertainty and fatigue, though, if you have a clear goal and a strong dedication. Recall that consistency is the foundation of habits. You go closer to establishing this habit as a vital part of your life every day you stick to your objective and every morning you wake up at five in the morning, reinforcing your dedication.

Making a mental change is another aspect of setting your intention. Try to regard waking up at five in the morning as a chance to take charge of your day, make investments in yourself, and design the life you choose rather than as something you must do. It will be simpler to persist with your early rising if it is more in line with your basic beliefs and objectives.

Gradual Adjustments to Your Sleep Schedule
You shouldn't abruptly change your schedule by many hours during the night just because you woke up at five in the morning. Actually, trying to make a significant change too soon can cause dissatisfaction, exhaustion, and possibly even disturbances to your body's regular cycles. Rather, the secret to making this transformation feasible and durable is to make little changes to your sleep routine.

The idea of waking up at 5 AM might be too much to handle if your usual wake-up time is closer to 7 or 8 AM. Start by progressively changing your wake-up time every few days in 15-minute increments to prevent systemic shock. This gradual change allows your body to get used to the new pattern, which facilitates the internal clock's adjustment.

For a few days, try waking up at 6:45 AM instead of 7 AM, for instance. Push your wake-up time to 6:30 AM, then 6:15 AM, and so on, until you get to your ideal wake-up time of 5 AM, once you feel at ease at that time. This gradual transition lessens the shock of the change and guarantees that you aren't pushing yourself into an unsustainable pattern.

You will also need to gradually modify your bedtime in addition to your wake-up time. To wake up feeling rejuvenated and invigorated, it's critical to make sure you're receiving enough sleep every night. You should try to get seven to eight hours of sleep a night, therefore you will need to change the time you go to bed. Try to get into bed by 9:30 or 10 p.m. if you are waking up at 5 a.m. Every few days, gradually move your bedtime up by fifteen minutes until you achieve the target bedtime, exactly like you do with your wake-up time.

In addition to guaranteeing adequate sleep, the progressive method allows your body to adjust to your new sleep schedule. The circadian cycle of your body has a big impact on how you feel in the morning. You can gently train your body to go to sleep and wake up at the right times by gradually changing your bedtime and wake-up time.

Overcoming the Initial Struggles of Waking Up Early
The initial challenges of rising up at 5 AM are unavoidable, regardless of your level of commitment. After just a few days of waking up early, your body might rebel against the new routine and the warmth of your bed might seem like an alluring haven. Although this uncomfortable phase is quite common, you may overcome these obstacles and maintain your new habit if you have the correct mindset and tactics.

The urge to use the snooze button is one of the first challenges that many individuals face. You can feel sleepy, exhausted, or reluctant to get out of bed in the early days of waking up at five in the morning. It's easy to get caught up in the thought, "Just five more minutes." However, using the snooze button can make getting out of bed even more difficult because it throws off your sleep schedule and makes you feel even more exhausted. To get around this, try setting your alarm clock such that you have to get out of bed in order to turn it off. This little movement can assist you get out of your groggy state and let your brain know it's time to wake up.

Feeling excessively exhausted during the day is another prevalent issue. Your body might not be accustomed to getting up early at first, and you can experience daytime fatigue. Establishing a nightly regimen that encourages relaxation and sound sleep will help you fight this and ensure that you're getting enough sleep. Before going to bed, steer clear of stimulants like gadgets and caffeine and think about including relaxing pursuits like reading or meditation. Your energy levels will gradually increase as your body adjusts to rising earlier.

Persistence is the key to getting past these early obstacles. It's critical to realize that developing a new habit takes time and that any initial discomfort is just momentary. It will get easier the more often you get up at five in the morning. Your body will eventually get used to rising early, and it won't feel like a hassle. Keep in mind that each day you overcome the challenges and get up early, you go closer to forming this habit as a lifelong one.

Consider the long-term advantages of rising at five in the morning to help you get over your early morning lethargy. It's easier to get past the early discomfort when you remind yourself of your clear aim and the benefits this new habit will bring to your life. Getting up early is an investment in your future success, regardless of whether you're pursuing a personal objective, increasing your productivity, or just looking for a better work-life balance.

In conclusion

Developing the habit of rising at five in the morning is a prolonged process that involves setting your aim, modifying your schedule, and overcoming any obstacles that may arise. Anyone may incorporate this effective habit into their daily routine if they have a clear goal and are dedicated to staying consistent. Your body and mind will have more time to acclimate if you start with tiny, reasonable steps. This will make the shift easier and more sustainable. As you persevere through the initial challenges, you'll discover that rising at five in the morning becomes second nature, giving you a better start to the day, increased mental clarity, and the chance to accomplish your objectives more quickly. You may fully utilize the 5 AM regimen and start enjoying all of its many advantages if you are patient and persistent.

CHAPTER FOUR

DESIGNING YOUR MORNING ROUTINE

Getting up at five in the morning gets you a good start on the day, but what you do after that can make the difference between a stressful and chaotic day and one that is productive and rewarding. Here's where your morning ritual becomes important. When done correctly, a well-planned morning routine can have a profound impact on your general well-being, productivity, and mental health. The power of rituals and routines, how to create a morning routine that suits you, and effective 5 AM routines that have enabled others to reach their full potential are all covered in this chapter.

The Power of Rituals and Routines
Routines and rituals are important because they can influence how the remainder of your day goes. Your mind is usually at peace when you get up early, but it can rapidly evaporate if you plunge right into the responsibilities of everyday life. A regimen can make all the difference in this situation. A healthy morning routine does more than merely pass the time; it facilitates a meaningful and intentional shift from sleep to waking. Because they establish consistency, routines are reassuring. Decision-making and the mental clutter that frequently accompanies it are eliminated when you know exactly what to expect from the moment you wake up. You approach the day with clarity and intention because you already know what you're going to do. For instance, you have

already planned what to do first and what to do next, so you don't need to think about those things. This improves your mental focus and lowers stress. By letting your body and mind know that you cherish the beginning of the day and are deliberate about how you spend it, a routine is also a type of self-care.

In instance, rituals add a level of purpose and attentiveness. Rituals are practices that are performed with focus and reverence, almost as a kind of sacred act. Rituals help concentrate your thoughts and emotions, whether it's journaling, meditation, or reading something that motivates you. They enable you to establish a profound connection with oneself, fostering an attitude of calm and thankfulness that permeates the entire day. Knowing the function of routines and rituals in your life will enable you to make deliberate decisions that support your objectives, regardless of whether you're the type of person who thrives on structure or who likes a more relaxed start to your mornings.

Crafting a Morning Routine That Works for You
Creating a morning routine that fits your goals and lifestyle is essential to making sure it works and lasts. Although there is no one-size-fits-all method, balance and intentionality are at the heart of any successful morning practice. The most effective routines support your physical, mental, and emotional health in addition to increasing productivity.

Start by deciding what your morning's main priorities are. What do you hope to accomplish in the morning? If you're a productivity-driven person, your routine may center on things like working out, reading, or making a daily schedule. You may incorporate journaling, introspection, or visualization into your morning routine if you're interested in personal development. Decide what you want to achieve in the morning and adjust your schedule accordingly.

Start by figuring out how much time you can actually spend on your morning ritual. The benefit of rising at five in the morning is that it allows you plenty of time before the rigors of the day start. However, your own preferences will determine how much time you devote to each activity. You have the option of a longer, more comprehensive routine that lasts 90 minutes or even two hours, or a shorter, more concentrated one that lasts 30 minutes. As you develop your practice, you can modify the amount of time spent on each component. Start with a schedule that feels sustainable and comfortable.

Including exercises that encourage balance is a crucial component of creating a morning routine. It's simple to become consumed by the need to be busy, but self-care and relaxation should also be a part of your routine. Think about including activities that support your mental, emotional, and physical well-being. For instance, you may meditate for ten minutes to clear your head, work out for twenty minutes to revitalize your body, and then eat a nutritious breakfast to fuel your body. In a similar vein, journaling may be a fantastic tool for introspection and for making good plans for the day.

Maintaining flexibility is just as crucial as organizing your routine around your priorities. Certain mornings might not go as planned since life is unpredictable. Instead of following a strict routine, give yourself permission to adjust to the situations that arise every day. Maybe you have an unforeseen obligation or wake up feeling more exhausted than normal. Your morning ritual should prepare you to deal with life's challenges, not make it more stressful. Finally, keep in mind that consistency is essential. You may incorporate the schedule into your life by being consistent, even if your mornings initially feel chaotic. It will eventually become instinctive. Every morning, set small, achievable goals and acknowledge your accomplishments. Don't give up if you veer off course. Just start over the following morning and keep improving your technique.

Examples of Successful 5 AM Routines
Let's examine some successful people's morning routines to get you motivated and give you an idea of what a good 5 AM routine might look like. While demonstrating that there is no one "right" method to start the day, these examples can help you organize your personal routine.

As an illustration, consider Apple CEO Tim Cook, who is notorious for rising around 4:30 AM. Cook works out, checks his emails, and plans his day in the mornings. His regimen is designed to help him keep ahead of his rigorous schedule and maximize output. He feels in control of his duties as a leader since he uses his peaceful early mornings to make decisions that set the tone for the day.

Another proponent of the benefits of early mornings, Oprah Winfrey, begins her day by practicing appreciation. Though she incorporates morning routines like journaling, meditation, and reading motivational books, Oprah gets up at roughly six in the morning. She establishes the tone for the remainder of her day and tackles obstacles with composure and attention by beginning her day with optimism. Her practice emphasizes the value of introspection and establishing an emotional tone for the day.

Benjamin Franklin, one of America's founding fathers, is credited with establishing a more well-rounded routine. Franklin woke up at five in the morning and spent a few minutes thinking about how he would make his life better that day. Franklin is famously quoted as saying, "Early to bed, early to rise, makes a man healthy, wealthy, and wise." After working out in the morning, he had a nutritious breakfast and spent some time reading and studying. He prioritized learning, productivity, and health while beginning his day with purpose and vigor thanks to this well-rounded approach to morning activities.

These illustrations highlight how effective 5 AM routines can differ substantially based on a person's ideals and objectives. Finding what works for you and sticking with it are crucial. Some aspects of these routines, like goal-setting, exercise, or meditation, may motivate you to incorporate them into your own, but keep in mind that your schedule should represent your own objectives and aspirations.

In conclusion
The process of creating your morning routine is transforming and personal. An organized and purposeful morning routine can enhance the benefits of rising early and position you for success. You can gain a deeper understanding of the advantages of rising early by creating a schedule that fits your objectives, values, and way of life. Making a morning that fits with your plans for the day is the aim, regardless of whether you opt for a focused, productive routine or one that include time for introspection and self-care. You will have the ability to change not only your mornings but also your entire life as you continue to hone and perfect your daily routine.

CHAPTER FIVE

HOW 5AM CAN IMPACT YOUR PERSONAL AND PROFESSIONAL LIFE

Your personal and professional life can undergo significant change if you can harness the peaceful power of the early morning hours. Getting up at five in the morning gives you a big advantage and provides you with a quiet place to concentrate on the important things. This chapter will examine how you might use the early hours to concentrate on your personal development, strengthen your career, and encourage the kind of in-depth work that will help you achieve your objectives.

Using the Morning Hours to Focus on Personal Growth
Giving you time to concentrate on personal development is one of the most significant ways that 5 AM may transform your life. At five in the morning, the world has not yet awakened. You are still hours away from being pulled in all directions by the demands of your day, including your family, employment, and social engagements. You have a peaceful, distraction-free time to take care of your body, mind, and soul at this holy season.

Personal development can take many different forms. For some, it is studying a subject they wish to become proficient in or reading a book that motivates them. For others, it can entail writing in a journal, overcoming obstacles in their lives, or establishing new objectives. Whatever your strategy, the benefit of rising at five in the morning is that you have the time to devote to these pursuits without feeling hurried.

A lot of successful people talk about how important it is to undertake self-improvement every day. By rising early, you're emphasizing the development that will eventually determine your future rather than merely forming a habit. Consider beginning each day with 30 minutes of reading, 15 minutes of meditation, or some time to think about your own goals for the day. Over time, these behaviors accumulate to produce tiny but significant advances toward becoming a better, more self-aware version of oneself.

Attending seminars and reading books aren't the only ways to grow personally. It also involves cultivating a mindset that promotes your success and happiness over the long run. You may set the foundation for this in the morning. You can check in with yourself by practicing thankfulness or introspection in silence. For what do you feel grateful? How far along are you with your objectives? What obstacles must you overcome today?

Instead of just responding to the pressures of life, these activities assist you in approaching each day with clarity and focus. They cultivate a mindset that promotes resilience, fosters ongoing development, and gives you the mental toughness to overcome any challenges that may arise. The benefit of 5 AM is that it provides you with the energy and mental space you need to deliberately pursue personal development without being sidetracked or overburdened by the remainder of the day.

Building a Stronger Career and Achieving Goals
Even while 5 AM can be a very private moment, it is also crucial for career advancement. You can work on your business or job in the mornings with a degree of concentration that is difficult to

attain in the middle of the day. You understand how valuable these early hours may be if you've ever tried to find time for job progress.

You can concentrate entirely on the task that supports your long-term career objectives when everyone else is still asleep. Getting up at 5 AM offers you the chance to develop your profession in a way that fits with your specific goals, whether that means reading industry-related content, picking up new skills, or planning for your next major project.

The biggest obstacle standing in our way of achieving our professional objectives is frequently time. A lot of individuals wish they had more hours in the day to work on their goals, but 5 AM gives you more time that is all yours. The secret is to know how to use them well. The calm and quietness of the morning enables you to focus more intently on the work that will get you closer to success rather than juggling or hurrying through activities.

If you are an entrepreneur, for example, you might set aside five in the morning to concentrate on your business plan, improve your product line, or create content for your website. By taking classes, honing your communication skills, or scheduling meetings with mentors, you can invest in your professional development during the morning hours if you want to progress in your job. The idea is that, unlike most individuals, who approach their workplace reactively, early mornings provide the time and space necessary to be proactive about their careers.

You can also do more throughout the day if you start at 5 AM. You create momentum that keeps you going throughout the rest of the day when you get up early and make the most of that time. You project an image of being proactive and organized by finishing your to-do list before the day becomes crazy. By adopting this perspective, you stop just getting through your workday and start actively influencing it.

Consistency is also necessary for reaching your goals and strengthening your career. You may work methodically, day by day, on your goals in the early hours without feeling overburdened. Whether it's through business growth, promotions, or a sense of success that boosts your confidence, you're investing in yourself every day when you wake up at five in the morning.

The Power of Quiet Time for Deep Work
The capacity to work deeply is among the most potent benefits of rising at five in the morning. Deep work is the kind of concentrated, undistracted effort that enables you to complete challenging assignments and achieve significant advancements. In our increasingly distracted environment, this type of labor is highly regarded, but it is also the most difficult to accomplish when balancing other obligations.

The world is calm when you get up early. There are no calls to answer, no emails to reply to, and no meetings to go to. This quiet time is a gift that lets you work uninterrupted on high-value, concentrated tasks. The quiet of the early morning hours enables your mind to function at its best, whether you're writing, producing, designing, or tackling challenging challenges. When distractions grow later in the day, you might not have the energy, attention, or clarity to complete your most difficult activities.

The ability to enter a state of flow is the power of calm time for in-depth work. Time seems to slow down while you are totally focused on your work. Your productivity rises and you accomplish more in less time when you are in a state of flow. This is best done in the early morning hours, when you can focus on your work without being distracted by the stresses of everyday life. You may perform at your peak during the morning hours, whether you're working on a significant project, learning something new, or solving a difficult problem.

It takes discipline to work deeply, and getting up at five in the morning fosters that discipline. It involves forming the habit of setting aside time for important tasks and eliminating outside distractions. You have total control over how focused you are in the morning silence. You can decide to spend time on long-term initiatives that need your whole concentration or start with the most difficult ones, when your mind is still clear. Your ability to focus at other times of the day will improve the longer you stick with this routine.

In a world that demands our attention all the time, it's tempting to undervalue the importance of uninterrupted time. But when you get up early every day, you build a solid foundation for productive work that advances your career and personal objectives. Your ability to solve issues, think creatively, and move closer to your greatest goals will increase dramatically as you begin to reap the rewards of working quietly and undistracted.

In conclusion
The value of 5 AM lies in how you use those early hours to change your personal and professional life, not just in getting up early. You may create the groundwork for a more satisfying existence where you continuously invest in yourself by concentrating on your personal development. Making use of the peaceful early hours allows you to concentrate on in-depth work that furthers your career and aids in your goal-achieving. You can work on your most critical tasks without interruption when you get up at five in the

morning, which makes it possible for you to proceed in a more successful, efficient, and purposeful manner. By committing to this early hour, you are committing to a life of purpose and advancement—one that promotes your long-term success and pleasure.

CHAPTER SIX

OVERCOMING COMMON CHALLENGES

Getting up at five in the morning can seem like a straightforward, life-changing habit, but like any big shift, there are drawbacks. Although there are unquestionably significant advantages to rising early, there are also challenges that you will probably face. This chapter attempts to provide you the means to overcome these obstacles and keep moving forward on your path to success, from morning fatigue and lack of enthusiasm to the difficulties of keeping consistency and modifying your routine when life throws you curveballs.

Combatting Morning Fatigue and Lack of Motivation
Morning weariness is one of the most prevalent issues people encounter when they start waking up around five in the morning. When you're not accustomed to waking up earlier, this exhaustion can feel particularly overwhelming, and it's simple to revert to the habit of pressing the snooze button or clambering back into bed for a few more minutes of sleep.

Establishing a strong foundation of proper sleep hygiene is essential to overcoming chronic weariness. Make sure your body is receiving enough sleep the night before if you're waking up at five in the morning. When people choose to get up early, they frequently undervalue the significance of having a regular bedtime. Try to go to bed earlier if you want to successfully implement 5 AM as your new wake-up time. It is essential to get 7 to 8 hours of sleep per night. You might need to change your nightly routine, which could include putting an end to screen time an hour before bed, turning down the lights, or making your bedroom more peaceful. It could take some effort to get rid of late-night habits like watching TV or browsing through your phone and replace them with a more relaxing bedtime routine.

You might also feel a little groggy or have trouble waking up completely in the early days of waking up around five in the morning. Especially if your body is getting used to a new rhythm, this might be typical. Your body will eventually get used to the new wake-up time, though, and you'll probably notice that mornings get easier. Make sure to drink water early thing in the morning if you feel especially lethargic because staying hydrated can help you overcome your drowsiness. Additionally, to get your blood flowing and stimulate your body, think about adding a little exercise to your morning routine. Fighting off that early morning lethargy can be greatly aided by stretching, walking, or even a short yoga session.

An additional issue that could ruin your 5 AM routine is a lack of drive. On days when you don't feel very motivated or thrilled, it can be simple to talk yourself out of getting out of bed when the alarm goes off. It's critical to understand that motivation by itself rarely results in long-lasting change. Make your 5 AM wake-up time a non-negotiable aspect of your routine instead, and concentrate on developing discipline. Clearly state your intentions for waking up at this particular moment. Whether your goal is productivity, personal development, or long-term objectives, having a clear purpose will help you overcome periods of low motivation.

Think about establishing modest, doable objectives every morning that complement your more ambitious aims. You give yourself a cause to get out of bed that is stronger than the fleeting comfort of staying under the covers when you wake up with a purpose, whether that be reading, writing, working out, or reflecting. Your drive will start to flow freely if you link your early mornings to worthwhile objectives.

How to Stay Consistent and Avoid Burnout
When it comes to rising early, consistency is essential. But it's simple to veer off course, particularly when life's responsibilities begin to feel too much to handle. For a few days, you might wake up at five in the morning, but on the fifth day, you end up pressing the snooze button. Being inconsistent can cause dissatisfaction and self-doubt, which makes it more difficult to get back on track. The most crucial thing to keep in mind in this situation is that forming a new habit requires time and that failures are a common occurrence. Establishing a schedule that is adaptable rather than strict is one of the best ways to keep things consistent. It's simple to assume that if you get up at five in the morning, you have to do a certain set of things every day. Routines don't have to be rigid, even though they can be quite helpful. Some mornings might not go as planned because life happens. Concentrate on consistency rather than perfection. Simply getting up early and setting out time for your goals, however flawed, will provide the constancy you require, even if you are unable to finish everything you had planned for the morning.

Controlling expectations is a crucial component of consistency. When you initially start getting up at five in the morning, it's simple to get excessively ambitious, but trying to do too much might result in burnout. Prioritize quality over quantity and keep your objectives reasonable. Too many activities or irrational expectations in the mornings can quickly sap your motivation and leave you feeling overburdened. As your morning routine gets more engrained, start small and work your way up. Recall that progress, not perfection, is the aim.

Another prevalent issue that frequently results from pushing oneself too hard is burnout. You could feel exhausted both physically and psychologically if you're pushing yourself too hard to reach your goals or if you're getting up early to do a long list of duties. This is particularly true if you don't get enough sleep at night or if your day is just a never-ending loop of work, stress, and fatigue.

It's crucial to include self-care in your early morning routine to prevent burnout. Schedule downtime for contemplation, mindfulness, or rest. Give yourself time to relax so that your mind and emotions can be rejuvenated. Keep in mind that the purpose of rising early is to create a balanced and satisfying life, not only to be more productive. The goal of your early mornings can be undermined if you overwork yourself. Maintaining a sustainable and regular 5 AM regimen requires taking breaks and paying attention to your body's needs.

Adjusting Your Routine During Life's Unexpected Events
Even the best-laid plans occasionally need to be modified since life is unpredictable. Your 5 AM routine may be disrupted by unforeseen circumstances, such as a health condition, a difficult project at work, or an unexpected family emergency. It's critical to have plans in place for remaining on course at this time without becoming overwhelmed.

Being adaptable with your routine is one of the finest strategies to deal with these interruptions. Even if you had intended to wake up at five in the morning every day, reality will occasionally force you to make adjustments. This implies being flexible as circumstances arise, not completely giving up the habit. Try to get up an hour later and allow yourself to make the most of that time if you are unable to wake up at 5 AM due to an emergency or a late night. Even an additional hour of sleep can occasionally significantly impact your energy levels, enabling you to recharge and resume your routine the following day.

Keeping a self-compassionate perspective is also crucial. The tension of feeling like you've failed at your 5 AM goal is added to the already stressful situation of life's unforeseen happenings. Recognize that failures are inevitable and that, after the commotion subsides, you can always go back to your early mornings. During these periods, be nice to yourself and understand that your ability to bounce back and keep going forward, rather than a few bad days, defines your long-term success.

Additionally, you might need to briefly reconsider your morning routine if you encounter significant disruptions. For instance, it might not be the best time to partake in high-intensity activities like a demanding workout or extended reading sessions if you're juggling a high-stress assignment or a personal problem. Prioritize what really matters in these situations; it could be journaling, meditation, or just spending some time to think and relax. Your routine's adaptability will let you change it to suit your demands at any time.

As you proceed on your 5 AM trip, it's critical to keep in mind that success is about developing a habit that benefits your life, even in the face of life's unpredictability, rather than about always adhering to a strict schedule.
In conclusion

Overcoming the difficulties of rising at five in the morning is a process rather than a final goal. At first, it's normal to feel exhausted and unmotivated, but you may get past these obstacles by maintaining discipline, focusing on proper sleep hygiene, and creating a flexible schedule. Avoiding burnout is just as crucial as being consistent. As you go, you'll discover how to modify your routine in response to unforeseen circumstances in life, preserving the harmony between wellbeing and productivity. The most important thing is to remain dedicated, treat yourself with kindness when you fail, and never forget why you started this trip in the first place. Getting up at five in the morning may become a life-changing habit if you have the patience, persistence, and adaptability to make it work.

CHAPTER SEVEN

TRANSFORMING YOUR LIFE THROUGH CONSISTENCY

Many people believe that consistency is the key to long-term success, and this is particularly true when it comes to rising at five in the morning. The consistency and commitment to incorporating this practice into your daily routine will have more long-lasting effects than the odd early rise. This chapter will cover the significance of monitoring your progress, acknowledging minor victories, and comprehending how early rising's compound effect can eventually drastically alter your life. We'll also look more closely at the testimonies of people who have changed their life by sticking to the 5 AM practice, showing that even modest, continuous action may have a big impact.

Tracking Progress and Celebrating Small Wins
The changes might not appear noticeable when you initially start waking up at five in the morning. Maybe you feel a little more energized in the mornings or like you've accomplished something when you finish your morning routine. However, if you don't take the time to monitor your development, these minor triumphs may easily go unrecognized. In actuality, the initial outcomes are frequently neither striking nor instantaneous. If you don't see results right away, it's tempting to lose hope, but if you learn to monitor your progress and acknowledge even the little victories, you'll gain the momentum you need to maintain this practice over

time.

Journaling is one of the best strategies to monitor your development. Spend some time thinking back on your morning at the end of each day. Did you get up as scheduled at five in the morning? When you got out of bed, how did you feel? What did you manage to get done in those early hours of the day? By writing down these thoughts, you start to document your experience, which enables you to see trends, areas for growth, and places where you might need to make adjustments. This feeling of responsibility might motivate you to stick to your promise and keep you on course.

It's also critical to acknowledge and appreciate your little victories. Your life will start to improve as you develop the habit of rising at five in the morning, whether it's through improved attention, more productivity, or a calmer start to the day. Even if these victories seem small, take a moment to recognize them. Celebrating your accomplishments gives you more self-assurance, reaffirms your dedication, and serves as a reminder that even little victories are worthwhile. Every little victory indicates that you're getting closer to your bigger objectives.

Reward yourself for maintaining your 5 AM regimen as well. Giving yourself permission to indulge in a simple treat, such as a warm cup of your favorite coffee, a stroll in the park, or even just taking a moment to unwind, can occasionally be a significant way to acknowledge your consistency. Expensive awards or large gestures are not always necessary. With these incentives, the early mornings will seem less like a duty and more like a chance for personal development.

The Compound Effect of Early Rising Over Time

The compound effect—the slow accumulation of minor gains that eventually result in significant change—is among the most potent effects of rising at five in the morning. When you first start a 5 AM routine, you might not experience any noticeable effects right away. You will, however, begin to reap the long-term rewards of your dedication to rising early as the days stretch into weeks and the weeks into months.

The foundation of the compound effect is the notion that little, regular actions add up over time. You are fostering an atmosphere that is conducive to achievement when you rise early every day. You position yourself for success in both your personal and professional lives by dedicating your morning hours to self-care, productive work, and personal development. Even while these little efforts mount up over time, they have a significant impact on your accomplishments, health, and outlook.

For instance, by rising at five in the morning every day, you make time for exercise, a nutritious breakfast, meditation, or concentrating on your top priorities. These steps will eventually increase your productivity, mental clarity, and physical well-being. On every given day, what can seem like a minor improvement becomes a component of a bigger change. The compound effect makes sure that your efforts compound in ways that are frequently only fully recognized months or years later, even though the consequences may not always be apparent right away.

Think about how it will affect your career. Early in the morning is a good time to work, brainstorm, and concentrate without interruption. Your capacity to carry out ideas gets better every day. These little steps forward will eventually add up to substantial professional advancements. This could be the drive to take on more tasks, the ability to complete a significant project ahead of schedule, or even the foresight to seek out new chances. You are giving yourself the gift of unbroken time when you invest in your mornings, and over the course of weeks, months, and years, you may notice improvements.

Productivity is not the only area where the compound effect occurs. It encompasses personal development as well. The early morning hours give you the chance to regularly partake in activities that promote personal growth, whether it's reading, writing, or goal-setting. You'll discover that these times of self-improvement have a long-lasting effect on your relationships, outlook, and general level of happiness. The real power of the 5 AM habit is found in the way it builds up over time, bringing about a cascade of constructive change.

Narratives of People Who Changed Their Lives by Adopting 5 AM
Those who have adopted the 5 AM habit and changed their lives have repeatedly demonstrated the effectiveness of early rising; it is not merely a theory. The tales of individuals who have made rising at five in the morning a key component of their success, whether they are well-known business owners or regular citizens, are encouraging and inspiring.

One such tale concerns Apple CEO Tim Cook, who is infamous for rising around 4:30 AM each day. Cook works out, reads, and responds to emails in the morning before everyone else gets up. His dedication to rising early has enabled him to keep a laser-like concentration on his professional and personal well-being, positioning him for success as the head of one of the most significant corporations in the world. Cook views the calm of the early morning as a chance to get ahead of the day and concentrate on his personal and professional obligations. His experience serves as evidence of the effectiveness of establishing the tone for the rest of the day during the first few hours of the day.

Oprah Winfrey is another example, since she has included rising early into her daily schedule. Oprah uses her mornings for meditation, introspection, and physical and mental exercise. She attributes her ability to remain grounded, organized, and goal-focused to her 5 AM wake-up hour. Oprah's dedication to rising early has allowed her to strike a balance between her demanding profession and personal development, finding time for significant self-care and creative endeavors. Her experience serves as a potent reminder that getting up early not only increases productivity but also promotes emotional and mental well-being.

Celebrities are not the only ones who have these stories; regular individuals who have decided to embrace the power of early rising have them running through their lives. Whether they are professionals, writers, or entrepreneurs, many successful people have discovered that the early hours of the morning provide them the energy, clarity, and focus they need to accomplish their objectives. For these people, rising early is an essential part of their personal and professional development, not merely a habit.

Think about Sarah, a small business owner who started getting up at five in the morning to concentrate on her marketing plan before the day's responsibilities took over. Her production significantly increased in just six months, enabling her to introduce new items and expand her clientele. Sarah's tale demonstrates how getting up early gives you the time and space you need to focus uninterruptedly on the things that matter most in your life. Making the most of your time and working smarter are more important than working harder.

In a similar vein, writer Michael discovered that his best work came in the early hours of the morning. He was able to devote unbroken time to writing by rising at five in the morning every day. As a result, he completed his first book in three months, something he had been struggling to do for years. Michael's success story serves as an example of how minor adjustments to your daily schedule, such as rising earlier, can result in major improvements in both your personal and professional lives.

In conclusion
The deep effects that waking up at five in the morning can have over time, in addition to the immediate changes that can be observed, are what give it its transforming power. Consistency is the key to success with this habit, and you will see little but meaningful gains in your life by monitoring your progress, acknowledging your accomplishments, and seeing the compound effect of your efforts. Early rising may genuinely transform lives, as seen by the success tales of those who have made it a pillar of their life. Waking up at five in the morning may be the key to realizing your potential and changing your life if you have the patience, commitment, and determination to stick with the process.

CONCLUSION

EMBRACING THE POWER OF 5 AM

It's time to consider what you've learned about the transformational potential of rising at five in the morning as this book draws to a close. It may not have been a simple transition from a late-night sleeper to an early riser, and there will undoubtedly be difficulties along the way. However, I want you to keep in mind that every significant shift starts with a single step as you stand on the brink of change. You now have the means to make this shift long-lasting, durable, and significant in all facets of your life, just as you have learned to appreciate the early hours of the morning.

The Long-Term Benefits of Waking Up Early
Better attention, increased productivity, and more time for self-care are some of the obvious and immediate advantages of rising at five in the morning, but the whole impact of early rising is not often immediately apparent. Although they may not be immediately apparent, the long-term advantages of rising early are significant and transformative. Having more time in the day is only one of these advantages. They affect all aspect of your life, including your relationships, work, mental health, and even your sense of purpose. Developing a sense of control over your life is one of the most significant long-term advantages of rising early. You are in a position of power when you awaken before the outside world asks you to do anything. Without other demands or distractions, you are free to choose how you want to spend those initial few hours. This sense of independence can help you feel more in control of your

future, lower stress levels, and boost your sense of self-worth. You have more time to think about your objectives, make plans, and arrange your day according to your bigger aspirations in the peaceful mornings. By doing this, you begin to feel as though you are in charge of your own destiny.

Additionally, getting up early encourages discipline and consistency, two qualities that are critical for long-term success. Consistently rising early gives your day structure and aids in creating a pattern that advances your objectives. You are developing the discipline to work toward your goals every day, no matter how tiny the steps may appear, by sticking to this program. This steadfast dedication to your daily routine will eventually create an irrepressible momentum. The self-control, perseverance, and persistent qualities you develop early in life are reinforced in various aspects of your life.

The significant effects that early rising can have on your health are an additional long-term advantage. Getting up at five in the morning encourages you to prioritize sleep by getting to bed at a sensible hour, even though sleep is necessary for healing your body and mind. This indicates that you will be obtaining adequate sleep, which will enable your body to repair, rejuvenate, and perform at its peak. You can improve your general health and well-being by letting your body know that rest and recuperation are vital by rising early. Additionally, the peaceful morning hours can provide time for exercise, which has both short-term and long-term advantages for your physical well-being, such as boosted vitality, elevated mood, and enhanced cardiovascular performance.

Over time, getting up early contributes to the development of mental clarity. Because everything around them is still quiet, early risers frequently feel more at ease and focused. This calmness helps to clear the mind and makes it possible to make more deliberate decisions. Your mind will have more room to think deeply, solve problems, and create if you set aside the early hours for meditation, introspection, or concentrated labor. You will be able to stay focused on your most crucial duties and objectives throughout the day thanks to this clarity.

The effects of early rising on your career are arguably among the strongest long-term advantages. You are setting yourself up for job success by getting up early and working hard throughout those hours. Your early morning activities will eventually add up to more creativity, productivity, and the capacity to finish more important tasks. Your capacity for time management, critical thinking, and idea execution will distinguish you from others and open doors to new opportunities, professional progress, and personal fulfillment.

Your Next Steps to Becoming a Morning Master
It's time to act now that you've witnessed the long-term advantages. To strengthen your resolve to rise early, the next steps in your journey are essential. Reading about the power of 5 AM is one thing, but experiencing it yourself is quite another. It's about putting your newly acquired information into practice and keeping moving ahead in the face of setbacks.

Being patient with oneself is the first step. Just as Rome wasn't created overnight, so too is the practice of rising at five in the morning. Don't be disappointed if you make a mistake, and don't anticipate perfection. It takes time to change, and it takes grace and self-compassion to form a habit as powerful as rising early. You just need to recommit and adjust if you find yourself missing a few early mornings. This doesn't mean your adventure is over.

Keep monitoring your development. Keep a journal or make a log in which you can document your daily feelings, reflections, and morning accomplishments. You'll see trends and advancements over time, which will sustain your motivation. You can stay going by celebrating the little victories when you keep track of your progress. The secret is consistency; the more you stick to your wake-up hour, the more organic it will feel.

Adapting your routine to your changing demands is another crucial step. Your morning routine might need to change as you go along. You might find that some things no longer work for you, or you might find that you pick up new routines or pastimes that improve your mornings. Don't be scared to make adjustments and changes to your routine to make sure it still supports your objectives and personal development. Make the early morning hours work for you in a way that feels motivating and empowering because, after all, they are for you.

Don't undervalue the importance of responsibility either. Talk to a mentor or a buddy about your trip. You are not alone in this. You can stay accountable and be more motivated if you have someone to check in with or celebrate victories with. Your dedication to rising at five in the morning may even encourage someone else to follow in your footsteps.

Lastly, keep in mind that the goal of your early mornings is to create an environment where you may flourish rather than merely be productive. The life you are creating—one in which you are in charge, have the time to devote to yourself, and are always developing—is reflected in your 5 AM routine. See every morning as a gift from God, and make the most of it by being your best self.

Final Words of Encouragement
Remember that you are starting a journey of great personal development as you take the last steps into this new chapter of your life. It's not always simple, and there will be times when keeping up the momentum seems difficult. Your greatest growth, however, will occur during these difficult times. Remember that each morning you get up early is a decision you are making for yourself in the future.

The path to mastery is paved with self-compassion, discipline, and consistency. You will start to realize how much of an impact it has on your life as you continue to wake up at five in the morning. You'll have greater energy, concentration, and time management skills. You'll be more productive and have more clarity in your thoughts. As you develop into the person you were always meant to be, you will feel a profound sense of fulfillment and be able to achieve more than you ever imagined.

The power of 5 AM is real; it can transform your life, increase your success, and foster personal development in ways you never would have thought possible. Therefore, adopt this behavior, have faith in the process, and keep in mind that you are growing into your best self every day that starts with an early rise.

I wish you luck on your travels. The world is waiting to see what amazing feats you will achieve.

www.ingramcontent.com/pod-product-compliance
Lightning Source LLC
Chambersburg PA
CBHW030512220526
45464CB00006B/2764